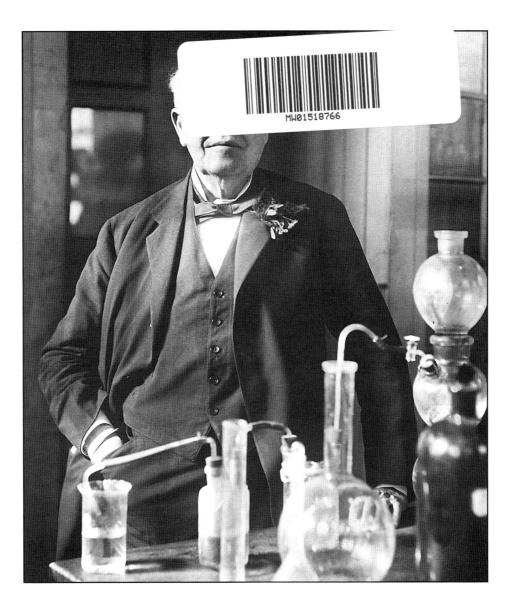

What's the Big Idea?
The Story of Thomas Edison

Have you ever had a good idea? Sometimes a good idea can lead to something big. Do you like to paint? Your good idea could become a picture. Do you like to write? Your good idea could become a storybook or a poem. Would you like to be an inventor? Your good idea could change the way people think, live and work.

In 1847, Thomas Edison was born. During his life, Edison had more good ideas than most people could keep track of. But when he was young, nobody thought he had any ideas at all. Nobody that is, but his mother.

Thomas Edison didn't talk until he was four years old. But he had been doing a lot of thinking. Soon he started driving everyone crazy with his questions. Other kids teased him.

Edison had trouble learning in school. His teacher was afraid he would not be able to learn.

When Edison was twelve, his mother noticed that he had trouble hearing. This didn't stop him from asking questions. Most of his questions were about science. His mother helped him set up his own science lab in the basement. But now his experiments smelled funny.

Edison's first job was selling newspapers and candy on the Grand Trunk Railway. One day he spotted a three-year-old boy crawling on the tracks. Edison pulled him away from a rolling train. He saved the boy's life. The boy's father offered Edison a reward.

People at railroad stations used the telegraph to send messages between stations. The operator needed a special keypad to send the messages. They used a new code called Morse code. A telegraph operator barely touched the "key" to send a short signal called a "dot." He held it down a little longer to send a "dash." Many dots and dashes made a word. A good operator could send Morse code messages almost as fast as he could talk.

Edison was very interested in Morse code. He knew what reward he wanted. He asked the boy's father if he could learn to use the telegraph!

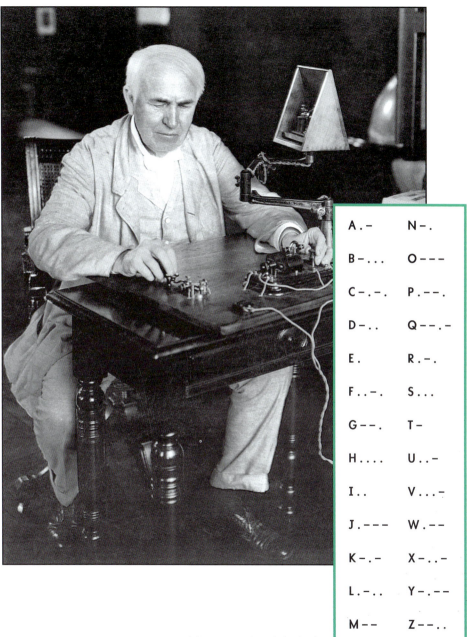

A.−	N−.
B−...	O−−−
C−.−.	P.−−.
D−..	Q−−.−
E.	R.−.
F..−.	S...
G−−.	T−
H....	U..−
I..	V...−
J.−−−	W.−−
K−.−	X−..−
L.−..	Y−.−−
M−−	Z−−..

Morse code alphabet

People had tried to invent ways to record sound. Edison had his own idea. He invented a way to record sound on cylinders coated with tinfoil.

Edison with a cylinder phonograph, 1878

One early model of a phonograph had two needles. One needle recorded sound. The other played it back. The first words Edison recorded were, "Mary had a little lamb." He knew it would work. Still, when he heard

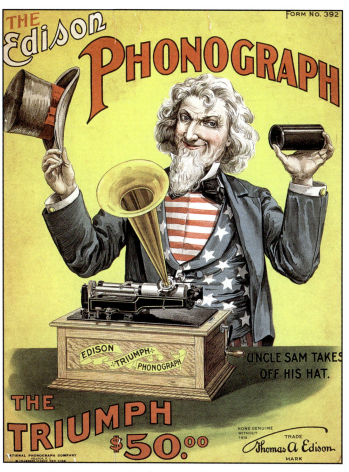

the other needle play the words back, even he was surprised.

Edison set up a company to sell his new machines.

Advertising poster for an Edison phonograph

Advertisement for Kerosene lamps

There was a time when there were no electric lights. People had to use a candle, an oil lamp or a gaslight to see at night.

Many ideas were tried to make electric light safe for the home. Edison thought of seven separate devices to make it happen. First, each device had to be invented. Then each one was carefully tested. He earned millions of dollars when he combined them.

The next step was to deliver electricity to people to power the new electric lamps. The first power station started up on September 4, 1882. It covered one square mile in downtown New York City.

Edison's electric lamp could be set up on a table.

Early electric street lights

Edison also invented the Kinetograph. This was the first camera that took movies. Now Edison needed a way for people to watch these movies. He invented the Kinetoscope. It lets one person at a time watch the movies made by the Kinetograph.

Kinetoscope invented by Edison

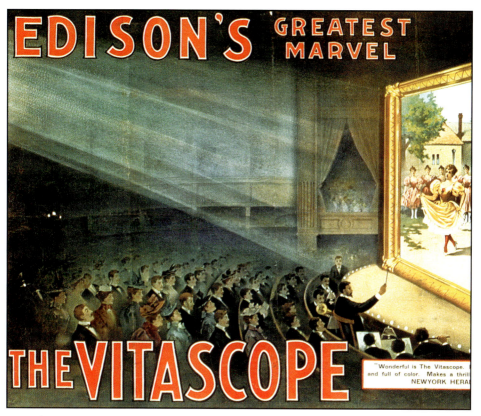

Advertisement used by Edison for the Vitascope

Next, Edison wanted many people to watch the same movie at the same time. He found a projector that showed movies on a big screen. It was called the Vitascope. Edison helped make and sell movies to use with the Vitascope. For the first time, many people could sit in a theater and watch a movie together.

Edison's laboratory in Menlo Park

Edison set up a laboratory in Menlo Park, New Jersey. He called it the "Invention Factory." People came from all over to work for him. He became known as "The Wizard of Menlo Park."

Edison was a tough boss. But working for him could lead to success. William Dickson worked for Edison. He got credit as co-inventor of Edison's movie camera.

Edison was not always easy to get along with. Inventions were his first love. Even so, he did marry and have a family.

Remember how much he liked the telegraph? He nicknamed two of his kids "Dot" and "Dash."

Edison called America's first movie studio the "Black Maria."

Not all of Edison's inventions turned out as he planned. Sometimes his inventions worked the way he wanted. At other times, he was surprised by the results.

During his lifetime, Thomas Edison created more than 1,000 inventions that were successful. He had many more that were not successful, but he kept having ideas and working on inventions.

Our lives would be very different if Thomas Edison didn't have his big ideas.